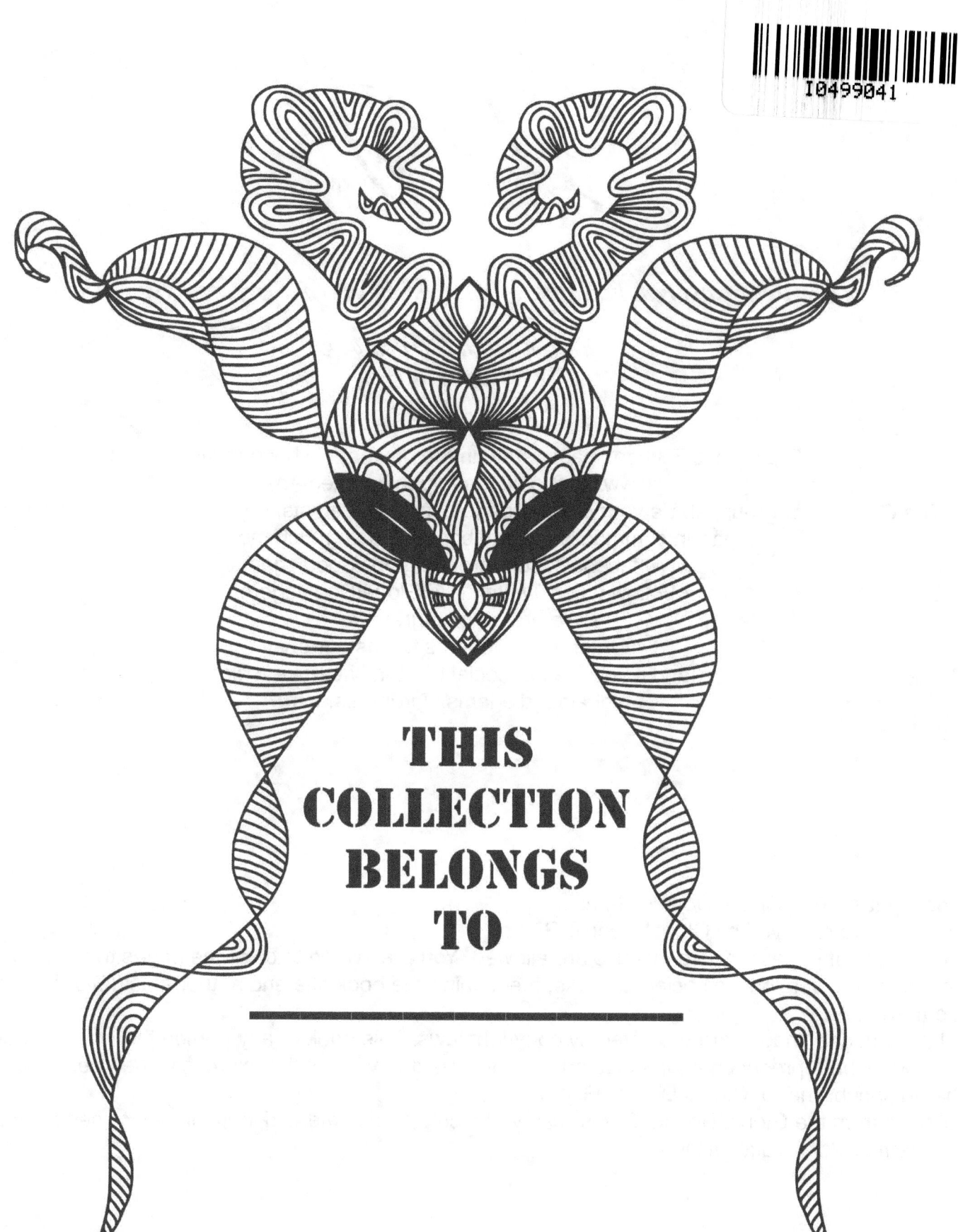

Share your colored versions with us ! We love seeing your results and hearing from you we are social !

The Official FB book page, stay on top of what we have in the works !
www.facebook.com/globaldoodlegems
The Community group, share your colored pages, meet the artists, enjoy exclusive freebies, take part in community Charity books and so much more......
www.facebook.com/groups/globaldoodlegems/
Follow us on Twitter.... @GlobalDoodlegem
We are on Instagram too
@globaldoodlegems for instagram
...and if you are not social like that we have a blog
globaldoodlegems.wordpress.com

Copyright © 2018 Global Doodle Gems
All rights are reserved by Global Doodle Gems.
Duplication of pages for personal use are allowed. You are invited to color the pages then scan/post your coloured versions to social networks, mentioning the book title and author/artist (Global Doodle Gems).
All artwork and images are protected by copyright laws. This book or any portion thereof may not, otherwise, be reproduced and/or distributed or transmitted without the express written permission of the artist/publisher of Global Doodle Gems.
All of us from the Global Doodle Gems wish you a colortastic time and look forward to seeing your wonderful color results online !

BugHead	Coming Through	Elephantasy

Here is looking at you !	Passionata	Simple Mandala

Squiggly	Weirdie'Dala Teaser of vol. 3 0501 2018	Twister from live drawing 26th Dec. 2017

Weirdie'Dala Teaser of vol. 3 1601 2018	Weirdie'Dala Teaser of vol. 3 1201 2018	From Weirdie'Dala's 3 not yet published...

YippieDippe Dahh	YomsieFlomsie	

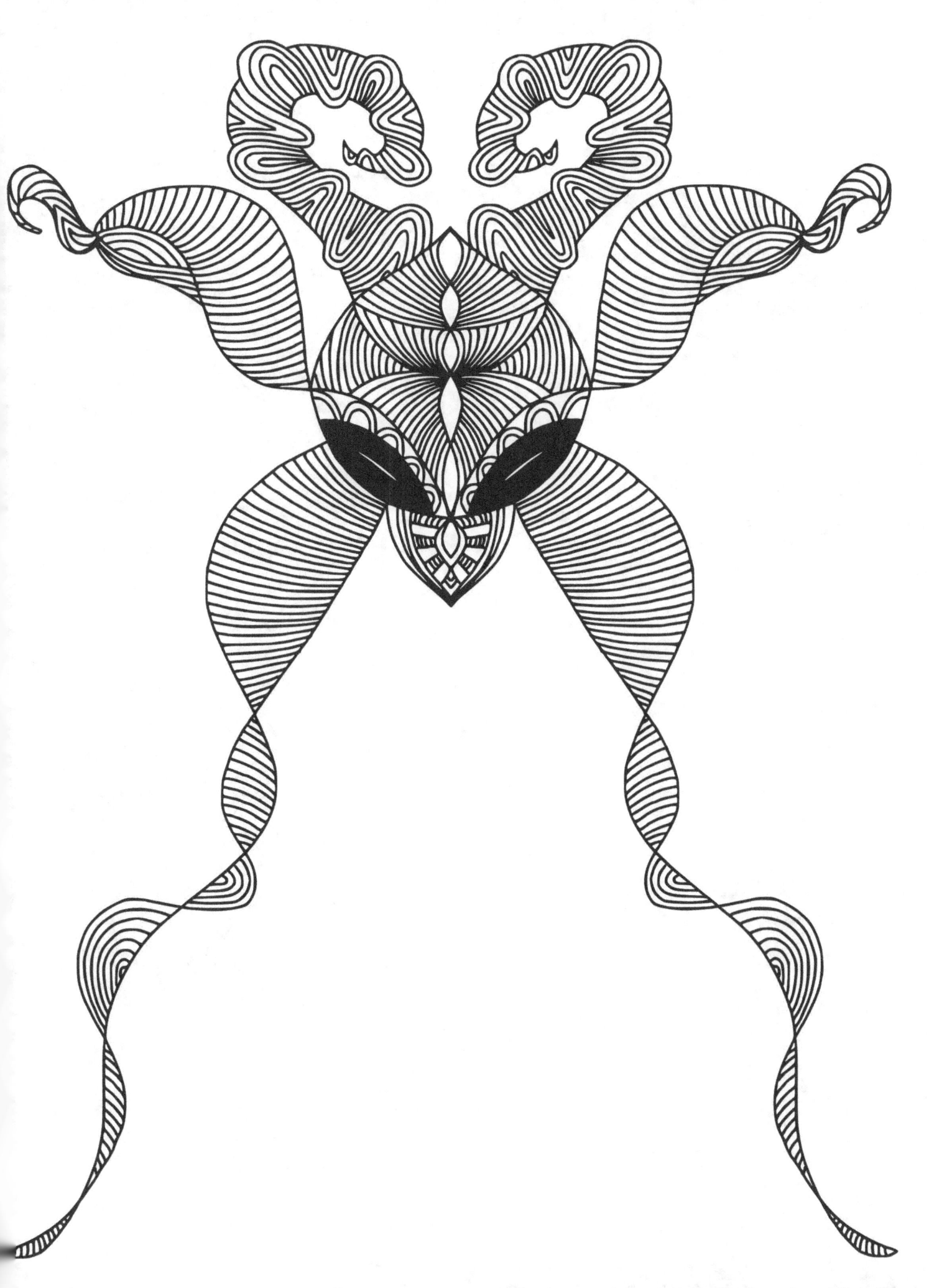

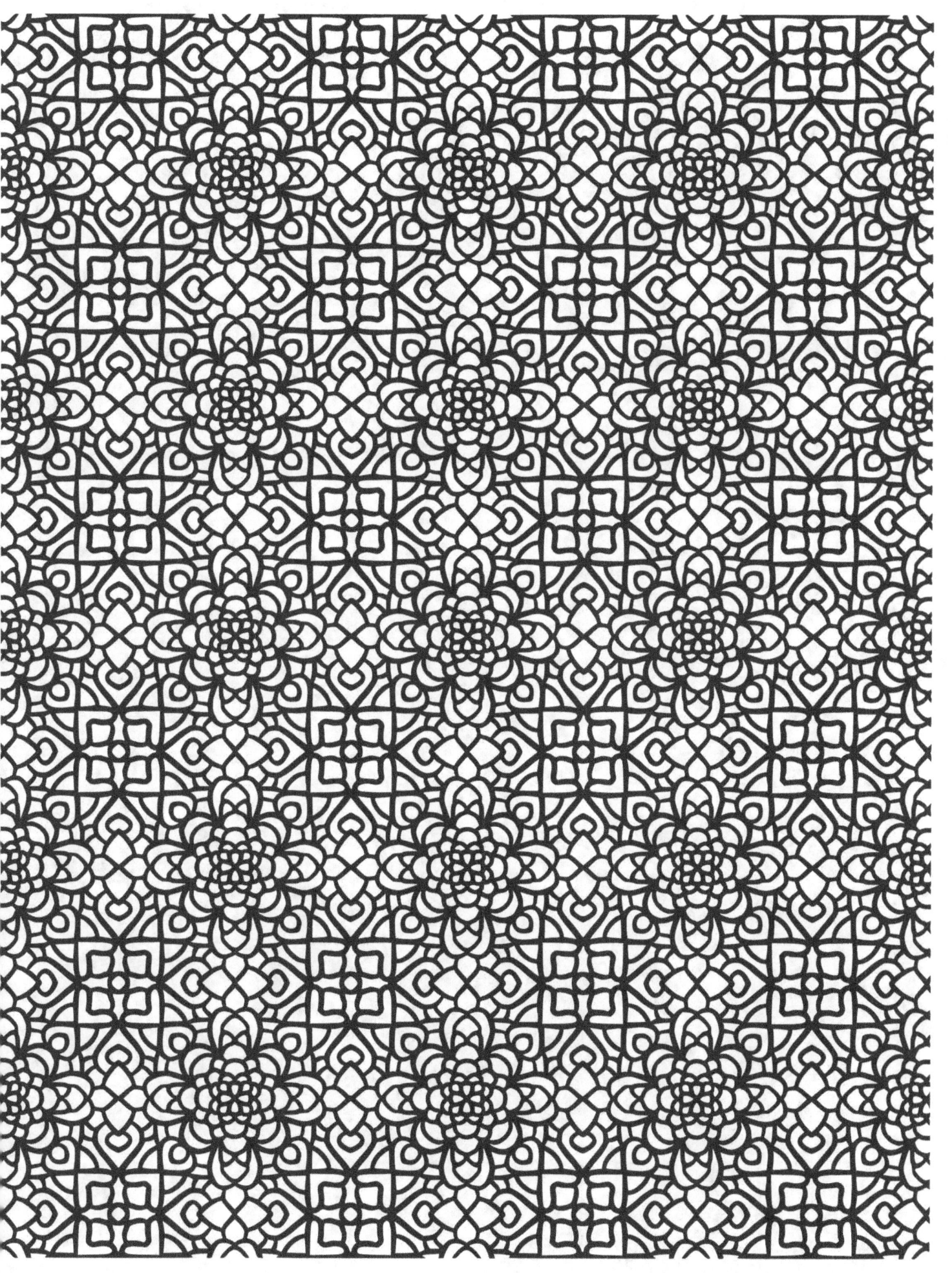

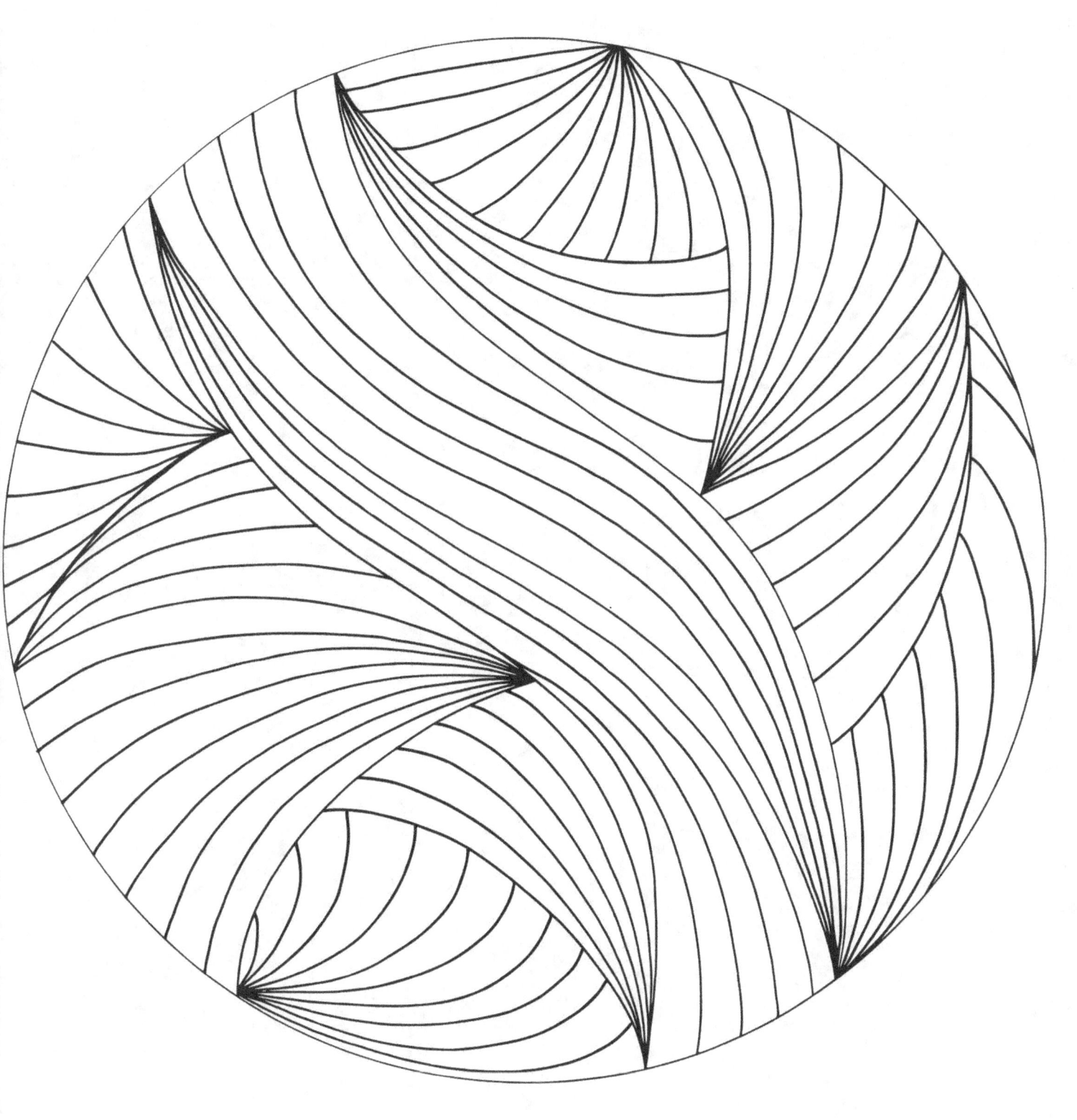

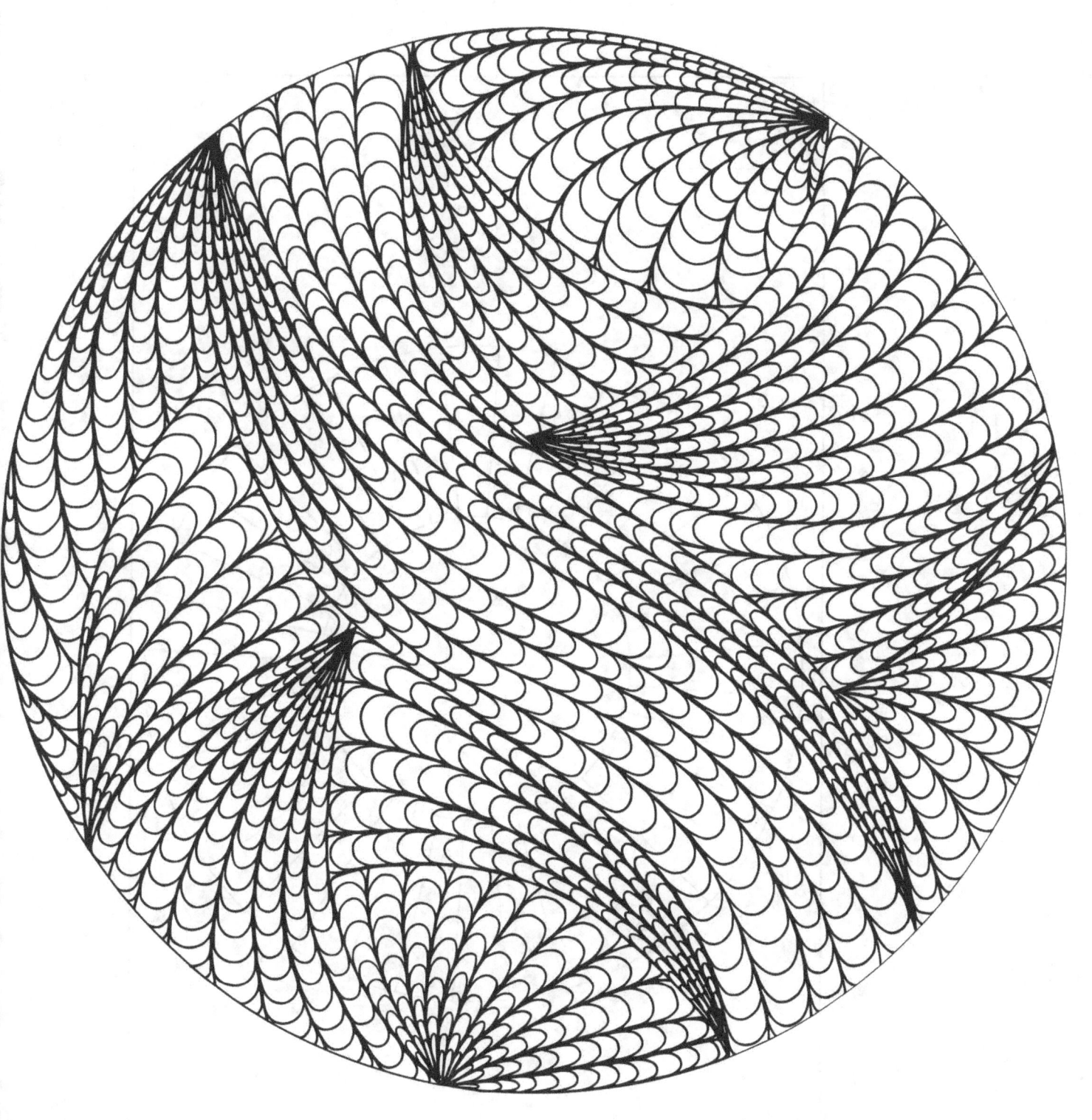

Test your colors here on the samples from
"My Pocket Coloring Companion"
&
"My Coloring Companion"

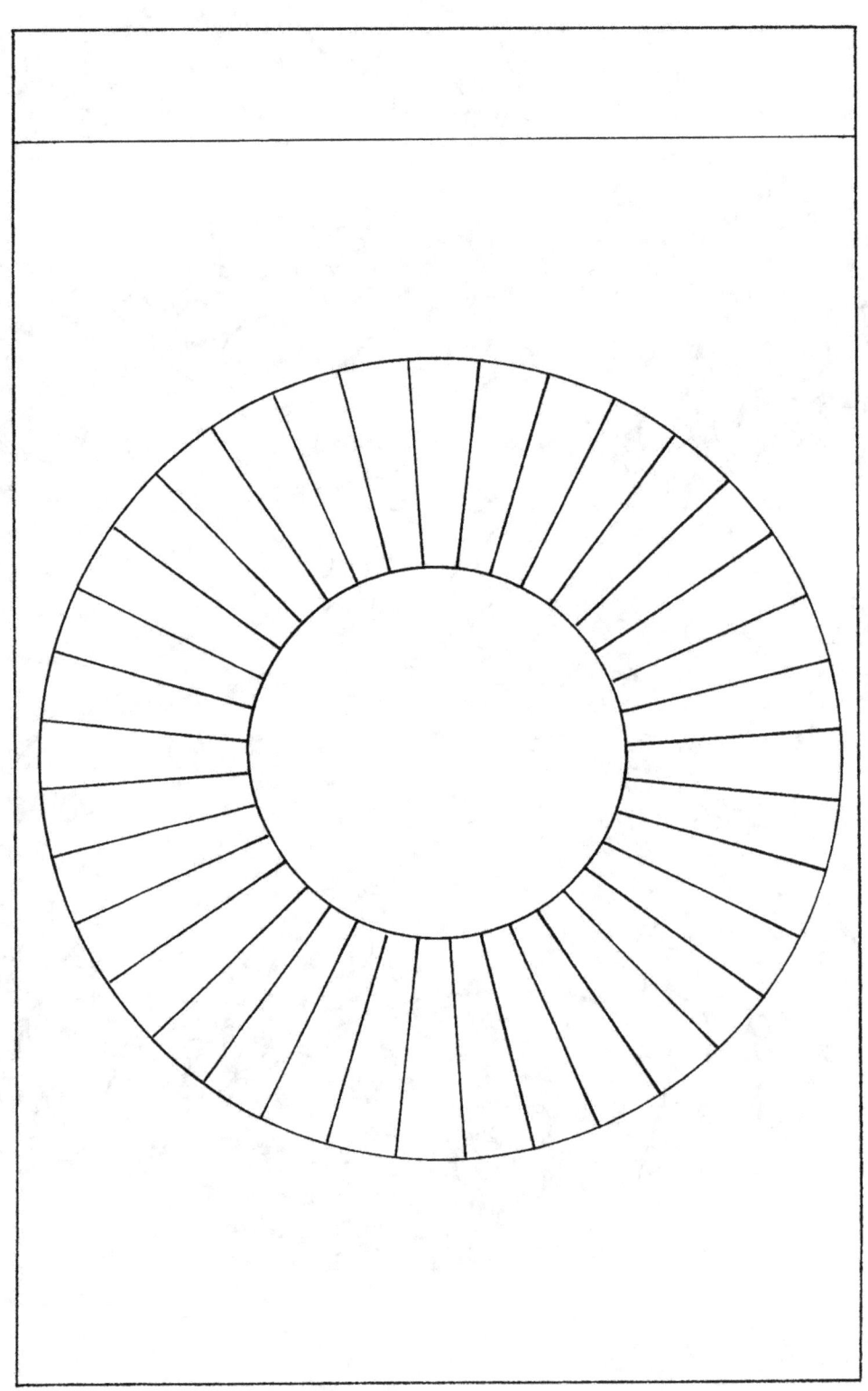

www.ingramcontent.com/pod-product-compliance
Lightning Source LLC
Chambersburg PA
CBHW082335220526
45470CB00008B/2512